THE
Archive Photographs
SERIES

PORTSMOUTH

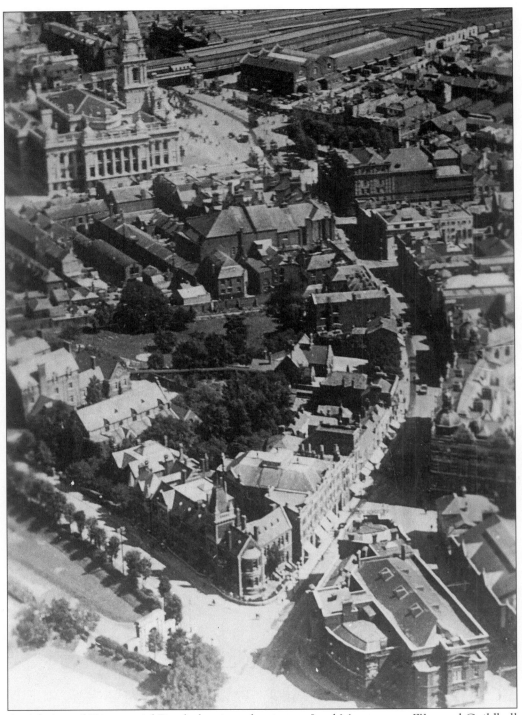

Aerial view of Commercial Road, showing what is now Lord Montgomery Way and Guildhall Walk, *c.* 1924. Pre-war landmarks visible here include the Hippodrome, the Board of Guardians' offices and, in the foreground, the Victoria Hall cinema.

THE
Archive Photographs
SERIES

PORTSMOUTH

Compiled by
John Sadden

CHALFORD

First published 1997
Copyright © John Sadden, 1997

The Chalford Publishing Company
St Mary's Mill, Chalford,
Stroud, Gloucestershire, GL6 8NX

ISBN 0 7524 0777 5

Typesetting and origination by
The Chalford Publishing Company
Printed in Great Britain by
Bailey Print, Dursley, Gloucestershire

To Mum in appreciation
and
In Memory of Dad
Thomas Lloyd Sadden (1919-1963)

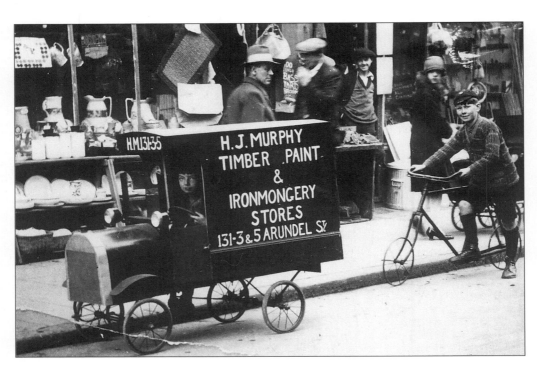

Contents

Acknowledgements

I would like to thank the following people for their help in researching this book and for their generosity in lending photographs and permitting them to be reproduced: Steve McCloskey, Geoff Wade and Portsea Island Mutual Co-operative Society Ltd., Bill Dick and the staff at G.A. Dick Ltd., Mr C.W.J. Savage, Dennis Stephens, Alan King and the staff of Norrish Central Library, Portsmouth City Libraries, Derek Dine, County Planning Officer Tim Greenwood and Hampshire County Council, Norman Shott, Mrs M.C. Sadden, Lord (Frank) Judd, City Engineer's Department, Portsmouth City Council, Gosport Library, Hampshire County Libraries, Doris Buick, Susan Sargent, Kirsty Williams, Jayne Fosbrook and the University of Portsmouth.

I would also like to express my special thanks to William Burbage, a remarkable man who has recorded with his camera many of the changes that have taken place in Portsmouth since the war. An ex-naval war veteran now in his eighties, Mr Burbage continues to take a lively interest in the city.

Finally, thanks to my wife Irene and daughter Karen for putting up with me and for being so patient while waiting to use the bathroom/darkroom.

Introduction

The two hundred people you see in the photograph on the cover of this book (reproduced in full on page 27) are witnesses of an historic event, though their faces give no hint of the importance of the occasion. Some are smiling for the camera, others are deep in conversation. There are top hats, bowlers, cloth caps, straw boaters and military and naval caps, suggesting that all classes are present. There is an elderly lady, born perhaps at the time of Waterloo and, in front of her, a small boy peering over the side of the barrier, who is young enough to still be alive today. Our link with history is so close and yet the past is, in L.P. Hartley's words, 'a foreign country where things are done differently'.

This book is a guide to that foreign country – to the Portsmouth that has passed – and the images you see here, which date from the last century right up to the 1970s, illustrate that things were, indeed, done very differently.

Perhaps the biggest and most dramatic influence on the appearance of our city this century – apart from war-time bombing – was the rise in popularity of the motor car. A novel form of transport affordable only to the professional classes eighty years ago, the car has become a personal necessity and symbol of individual freedom. Its convenience is appreciated by us all, but it is debatable if our overall quality of life has improved as a result. Traffic-free streets were relatively safe places for children to play, as the photographs in this book testify. Other photographs show local streets where communities have been devastated by road schemes. Today, children are driven to school because of the threat posed by traffic and it is reported that one in seven suffers from asthma or other respiratory problems. Will future generations look at digitalised photographic compilations of our traffic-clogged streets on their PCs and shake their heads in disbelief at our irresponsibility?

The contribution made by photographers to our understanding of the changing topography of our city, the flux of everyday life and the transient fashions of our grandparents is immeasurable. But its value extends beyond the historical to the evocation of those memories and emotions that personal recognition brings. We alone are experts of our own experience and if our memory is good then we are able to share our knowledge and experience with others. When our memory starts to fail then a photograph can prompt that joy of recognition and help stem that ebbing of the past.

But photographs ultimately deceive. They can lie literally, as in Southsea photographer Stephen Cribb's superimposed hydroplanes on p. 124. And, more obviously, photographs deceive by omission. For example, a view of sailors playing draughts in Portsmouth, pictured here on p. 42, might suggest to us that, after several months at sea, sailors typically enjoyed nothing better than a good game of draughts when they arrived back in port.

Similarly, we cannot expect the commercial photographer of the past to have represented common phenomena such as poverty or grim working conditions. Subjects were almost invariably selected according to their sales potential and so crowd scenes, main streets, business establishments and group portraits figure prominently in their work. There is, however, much to be discovered in the detail. The photograph of a shoe-less boy in Edinburgh Road which appears on p. 59 was blown-up from a street scene. Old photographs, then, can tell lies and reveal truths.

But interpretation skills are not needed to enjoy simply looking at how things once appeared to be. In the magical world of the photograph, long lost buildings remain standing; favourite pubs never call 'time'; the final curtain never descends at the theatre; fondly remembered corner shops remain 'open all hours' and the local church remains standing, eternally. The minutiae of everyday life is fixed in context in time. Fresh faces, which will never wither, gaze quizzically through the lens at us. And Pompey, pictured here on p. 83, hold the FA Cup in perpetuity.

Thanks to professional photographers like Stephen Cribb and gifted amateurs like William Burbage, we are able to enjoy the diversity and bustle of Portsmouth trade, from market totters to a bespoke tailor's and from a high class grocery store to old Ben Grubb's Government Surplus. And thanks to maritime photographer Edgar Ward we are able to dip our toe in the sea at Southsea in the days when it was safe to do so.

Happy paddling!

John Sadden, April 1997

One
Municipal Matters

The heart of Portsmouth's proud civic heritage, *c.* 1913. The old Town Hall was built between 1886/90, the Municipal College between 1904/08 and the 'jewel in the crown' of the city's landscaped gardens, Victoria Park, was opened in 1878.

Town Hall Council Chamber, c. 1910, the setting for many lively democratic debates until the Town Hall was effectively destroyed by the Luftwaffe on 10 January 1941.

Portsmouth Independent Labour Party Executive, seen here on the steps of the Town Hall, c. 1912. In the centre, sixth from the right, is Jimmy MacTavish, a dockyard shipwright, who fought against corruption in the Council and was a passionate advocate of working people's access to higher education. In 1915 he became General Secretary of the national Workers' Educational Association, an organisation which was especially strong in Portsmouth due largely to MacTavish's efforts.

Mayor John Timpson leads a lodge of ex-mayors into the parish church of St. Thomas's (now the Cathedral) in 1918.

Portsmouth Power Stations, 1963. Portsmouth was the first local authority to employ a steam turbine in its power station, which began generating electricity for the population in 1894 (see also p. 94). On the left is the Masonic Hall, which was originally built as the headquarters of the Portsmouth & Portsea Literary and Philosophical Society in 1831, but was sold to the Freemasons in about 1860 and demolished in 1963.

Lord Judd of Portsea, 1974. Frank Judd was MP for Portsmouth West from 1966/74 and for Portsmouth North from 1974/79 and is recognised throughout the City by people of all political persuasions as being the best and most hard working MP Portsmouth has ever had. His accessibility, both at his advice centre and on his regular visits to offices, factories, clubs, hospitals and old people's homes, is legendary. His constituents knew that once he had taken up a case he would genuinely do everything he could to help. He championed the cause of the underpaid, homeless and the unemployed and was a great believer in community values. Ennobled in 1991, Lord Judd is an expert on Third World issues and has served as Director of Oxfam and Voluntary Services Overseas. He was made a Freeman of the City in 1995.

Construction of council flats in Queen Street, c. 1958. Following war-time bombing and increasing expressions of concern that people were housed in conditions that were 'a mockery to civilised living', Portsmouth Council embarked on an impressive council house building programme. By 1949, Portsmouth ranked 7th out of nearly 1500 local authorities in the provision of permanent dwellings. One in 25 of the new houses was allocated to sufferers of tuberculosis, a disease which had previously been aggravated and spread by privately rented slum housing.

Refuelling of
Corporation refuse cart
in the 1920s.

Refuse collection in Campbell Road, *c.* 1910.

The Vicar of Portsmouth, the Revd E. P. Grant was the driving force behind the setting up of the Portsmouth and Gosport School of Science and Art in Pembroke Road in about 1870. His aim was to provide 'instruction in these two most important branches of education for all classes in the borough'. In 1894, the renamed Municipal Technical College moved to premises in Arundel Street, but its popularity was such that a larger, purpose built Municipal College was built on the Mayor's Lawn behind the Town Hall.

The laying of the foundation stone of the Municipal College and Free Library by Mayor J. E. Pink on 22 July 1904.

The completed Municipal College and Free Library, shortly after its opening on 10 September 1908. The architect was G. E. Smith, whose other local work included South Parade Pier and the R.N. School of Physical Training (see also p. 120).

Classroom interior of the old School of Science and Art in Pembroke Road.

Lending department, Central Library, 1930. In this year, Portsmouth libraries had 25,430 readers and issued 649,600 books. A librarian has described how the staff gave some of the readers nicknames appropriate to their habits: 'there was Weary Willie, Fidgety Fred, Peter the Ponce, Simple Sidney, Johnny the Creeper, Old Bill and Big Bertha.' Some of these regulars brought with them 'the nimblest of fleas with hearty appetites and a strong migratory instinct'. The staff's charity towards these borrowers was 'apt to wilt in the face of their rude behaviour and malodorous garments'. The library service was and continues to be appreciated by the vast majority of the population, though this was not always the case. It took over thirty years to convince the ratepayers of Portsmouth of the social and educational value of having a public library in the town. By 1883 the argument was won and a reading room was set up in a vacant building in the area where the Guildhall now stands. The spread of education and literacy led to a demand for more libraries and branches were opened in Southsea in 1893 and North End in 1897. By 1908, the new Central Library had been constructed as part of the new Municipal College and further branches were opened in Milton in 1925, Cosham in 1935 and in Copnor and Paulsgrove. The present Norrish Central Library was opened in 1976.

A chapter of librarians at the Central Library, *c.* 1920. Back row: Miss Burgess, Miss Bennett, Miss Priest, Miss Painter. In the middle is Miss Farrar. Front row: Miss Roper and Miss Sivell.

The Carnegie Library in Fratton Road which opened in 1906. The architect was A. E. Cogswell, best known as a pub designer for Portsmouth's breweries from the 1880s to the First World War.

A librarian and borrower pose for the camera in the Central Library to demonstrate 'business as usual' during the fuel crisis of 1947.

Post-war rebuilding of the Guildhall in February 1957. A crowd estimated at 20,000 gathered in the Guildhall Square for community singing after the Queen reopened the building in June 1959.

Boarding a tram at Clarence Pier, *c.* 1910. In 1901, Portsmouth Corporation bought the tramway system from the Provincial Tramways Company when it became clear that a privately operated company was unable to provide an adequate passenger transport service for the town's growing needs. Following municipalisation, the system was electrified, and tram car 84 (seen above) was one of the last of the old horse trams to be converted to electric operation. The electric trams proved very popular and profitable, leading to extensions to the system. The first motorbuses were used in 1919 to complement the service and by 1934 trolley buses had been introduced. The last tram ran in the City in November 1936. By the late 1950s, the trolley bus, which had come into its own during fuel rationing, began to be replaced by new motor buses and 1966 saw the beginning of the end of the bus conductor when all vehicles were equipped for one-man operation. The passing of the 1985 Transport Act ended the operation of transport as a public service by stripping local authorities of its control.

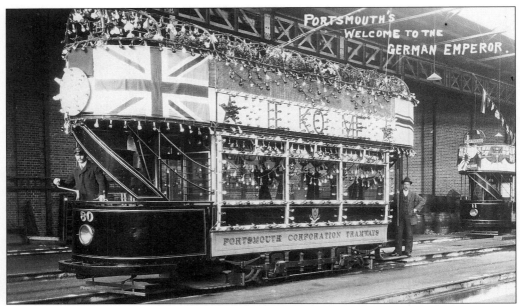

Tramcar 80 in North End Depot, photographed by tram driver J.L. Seekings in 1907. The tram is illuminated to welcome Kaiser Wilhelm who visited Portsmouth that year.

A trolley bus passes before a bombed-out Guildhall, a reminder of a later German visit. On the right is the war memorial.

Rare view of the interior of Portsmouth Police Court, *c.* 1910.

Portsea Police Station, *c.* 1860, which was believed to have been built in St. George's Square in the 1840s.

Victoria Park, *c.* 1906. Up until 1878 there were no parks or recreation grounds in Portsmouth except for a private playing field in Southsea and Southsea Common, which was owned by the War Office. The social and community benefits of public open spaces were finally recognised when pressure from Alderman E. Emanuel and Cllr John Baker and other pioneers led to the purchase of several acres of War Office land for a 'People's Park'. Victoria Park was opened to the public in April 1878 amid great celebrations.

Queen Alexandra Hospital, *c.* 1930. Opened in 1908 as a military hospital, 'QA' was taken over by the Ministry of Pensions in the 1920s to care for disabled First World War servicemen. The first civilian patients were treated during the Second World War and the Ministry of Health assumed responsibility for the running of the hospital in 1951.

Borough of Portsmouth Lunatic Asylum, *c.* 1904. Opened in 1879, it was renamed Portsmouth Borough Mental Hospital in 1920, became St. James' Hospital for Nervous and Mental Diseases in 1937 and St. James' Psychiatric Hospital in 1960, its changes of name reflecting the shifting attitudes to mental illness this century. The 'Care in the Community' policy will enable developers to build on much of the original 77 acre site.

St. Mary's Hospital, *c.* 1932. The East Wing can be seen above Milton Road. The Maternity Block was built in the 1960s on the cultivated area in the centre of the photograph.

Bombsites east of Commercial Road (now Guildhall Walk), 1957. The Theatre Royal is visible on the left.

Reconstruction work, 1972.

Two

In Defence of
the Realm

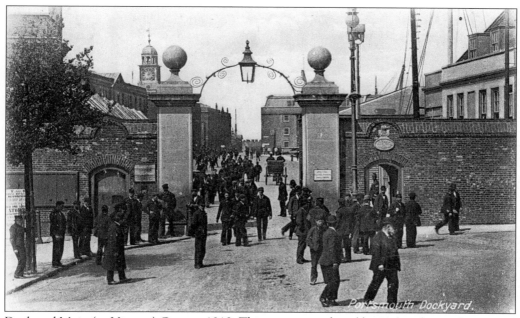

Dockyard Main (or Victory) Gate, c. 1913. This gate was widened by 12 feet during the Second World War to allow large loads and military vehicles to enter.

Dockyard workers leaving work via the Unicorn Gate, *c.* 1910. Built in 1778, this was one of the original gateways into the town of Portsea.

Marlborough Gate and Marlborough Row. By the 1930s, bicycles had evidently become popular with Dockyard workers.

Spectators at a Dreadnought launch, 19 August 1910. King Edward VII is dead and the naval arms race with Germany continues unabated. The occasion is the launch of the dreadnought-style battleship HMS *Orion* from the stocks of Portsmouth Dockyard, the fifth of nine to be built there. Four years after this crowd gathered to celebrate its launch, the great arms race culminated in the First World War.

HMS "NEPTUNE" AFLOAT IN PORTSMOUTH HARBOUR.
THE COLOSSUS OF THE WAVES."

The launch of the fourth dreadnought-type battleship HMS *Neptune* in 1909 provides a boatman with an urgent incentive to keep rowing.

PORTSMOUTH DOCKYARD
AND WARSHIPS.

HMS *Victory* (visible on left) was towed from Portsmouth Harbour into dry dock in 1922 for restoration. This view dates from the mid 1930s.

The great Double Ropehouse, 1,030 ft in length, dominates this aerial view of the Dockyard, looking east. The 50ft tall wooden clock tower and cupola on No. 10 Storehouse was destroyed by an incendiary bomb in 1941, but was restored in 1991.

First World War Dockyard munition workers, Electrical Engineer's Department.

Munition worker at a bench in the Electrical Engineer's Department, during the First World War. The first women to enter the very male world of the Dockyard had to run the gauntlet of abusive taunts and jostling and some took to carrying umbrellas to defend themselves. But soon the threats subsided as everyone rolled up their sleeves to fight a more pressing war.

The Royal Marine Light Infantry Dockyard Guard, pictured at R.N. Barracks in January 1916. All these men were pensioners and were proud of the 381 good conduct badges they held between them.

This 15 inch Howitzer at Eastney Royal Marine Barracks was used for training purposes. A complex system of pulleys and tackle was used to swing the heavy shells into the breech.

The Officers' Mess, Royal Marine Barracks, seen here *c*. 1910, was built at the west end of the parade ground in the 1860s.

Sporting heroes, stuck on the wall in the corner of a barrack room at Eastney, bring a personal touch to a cold and regimented environment. This photograph was taken in the 1900s by Mr Blake, who turned up at the Barracks every Sunday to take portraits for marines and band boys to send to their family and loved ones. Known as 'Blakey', he was distinguished by his very red nose.

R.M.A. Canteen at Eastney Barracks, *c.* 1910, taken by Mr. Blake.

Royal Marine Artillerymen enduring physical drill at Eastney, *c.* 1897. Long Barracks, on the northern side of the parade ground, was built in the 1860s.

Royal Naval Recruiting Office at the Hard, undated. This building served as a recruiting office and the Water Police Headquarters from the 1880s to the early 1920s and is now a tourist information office (see also p. 60).

Seamen and stokers awaiting inspection by the Lords of the Admiralty at Portsmouth Dockyard, *c.* 1899.

New Gas Kitchen at HMS *Excellent* Gunnery School, Whale Island, *c.* 1907.

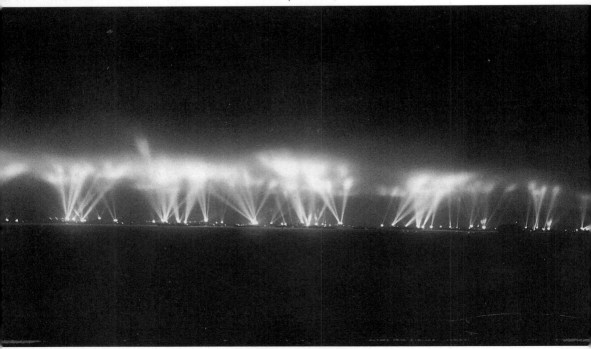

Searchlight display in the Solent, taken from the Esplanade at 10.30 on the evening of the 18 July 1914, during the Fleet Review. War was declared two weeks later.

Rare view of interior of armourers' workshop, HMS *Vernon* Torpedo School, undated. *Vernon* was transferred from amongst a group of hulks in Portsmouth Harbour to the Gunwharf in 1923.

Rare view of firing practice from one of the Solent forts, *c.* 1910.

The first house on Whale Island, under construction in 1864. The Island had been sold to the government three years earlier for £1,000 and HMS *Excellent* Gunnery School transferred ashore.

No-Mans Fort, *c*. 1910. The gangway can be seen on the right, the searchlights are silhouetted against the passing yacht and the guns are on the other side.

HMS *Excellent* Ammunition Room, *c.* 1910, which was housed in the building seen below.

Parade on the 'Quarterdeck', Whale Island, *c.* 1896. Men paraded twice daily before being marched off to their gunnery classes to the sound of a bugler.

Gunwharf Small Armoury, *c.* 1900. This housed many historic arms used at sea, including muskets, bayonets, cutlasses and pikes. Suits of armour are visible in the windows.

Not a comment on the British Fleet after the latest defence review, but a model of HMS *Powerful* made by a member of HMS *Vernon* Cycling Club, *c.* 1899.

Royal Marine Artillerymen with field guns at Fort Cumberland, *c.* 1907.

Earlier view of marines manning a 12 pounder field gun at Fort Cumberland, *c.* 1897.

CANADIAN ARTILLERY VISIT TO PORTSMOUTH 26 AUG 1911   SILK.

Visit of Canadian Artillerymen to Portsmouth, August 1911. The men were entertained by Mayor Alderman Scott-Foster at the Town Hall. They were congratulated on being 'typical sons of Greater Britain' and on their 'keenness with the gun' which was 'characteristic of the hardy race they represent'.

Troops depart from Cosham Railway Station *en route* to the Boer War via Southampton Docks, 1899. Hundreds of local sailors marched from their barracks to see them off.

40

First World War rally in Town Hall Square, August 1915. An estimated crowd of 100,000 gathered for this patriotic event.

Recruitment rally in Town Hall Square, August 1915. Famous French actress and pin-up Gaby Deslys used a 'bewitching smile and a few sentences of broken English' to appeal for recruits.

Duchess of Albany Home for Soldiers and Sailors, *c*. 1910. Between 1951 and 1972 this building was home to Agnes Weston's Royal Sailors' Rest, but has recently been rebuilt as the Portsmouth Foyer, a centre to help the homeless and unemployed young people of the 1990s.

View of General Recreation Room in the Royal Naval Barracks, *c*. 1912.

Anti-aircraft guns were positioned on Southsea Common in the summer of 1938 and a *Tiger Moth* was hired from Portsmouth Airport to fly up and down the seafront as a mock target. According to one of the Territorials who manned the guns, Raymond Hoar, crews relied on a series of John Player cigarette cards to distinguish RAF from enemy aircraft. A direct hit from an enemy bomber killed fourteen men in March 1941.

Group of Portsmouth firefighters and ARP (Air Raid Precautions) wardens, *c.* 1940. Copnor ARP warden Christopher Guy is on the right. Wartime bombing destroyed or seriously damaged nearly one fifth of properties in the city. 930 civilians were killed and 2,837 injured.

March-past at Hilsea, undated. Aside from the services, women took on many roles on the Home Front, including ARP warden, ambulance driver and firefighter.

Portsmouth's first khaki wedding of the war, St. Michael's Road Register Office, 22 September 1939. Gunner Dennis Stephens married Bette Dingle, having brought the date forward because of the war. Dennis manned the guns on Horse Sands Fort, while Bette was a cook for the Royal Engineers at Burnaby Road. The happy couple passed through a bridal archway of cooking utensils and were together for fifty-seven years.

Three
Street Life

Watching the world go by in Britain Street, *c.* 1935. A polished doorstep was a sign of respectability, even in slum ridden areas like Portsea.

Bonfire Corner, Portsea, in the 1940s. On the corner is Harkin's the tobacconist, next door to Smith the Barber, who later moved to Queen Street.

Mile End Post Office in 1971, shortly before its closure and the extensive redevelopment of the area.

Corner of Frederick Street, in the 1940s. Next to Smith the Barber is Paynes fish and chip shop and, at No. 17, George Brown the greengrocer.

Remaining shops in old Commercial Road, looking towards Lake Road, c. 1960. Fruit and vegetable merchants Richards, Gilhams, Hills, Cook, Ockenden, Pratts and Surridge dominated trade in this area.

Commercial Road and 'Landports', *c.* 1957.

Commercial Road, July 1957 (see p. 100).

Commercial Road, 1970. The Air Balloon pub and Flying Bull Lane School are on the left.

Shoppers in Guildhall Square in the summer of 1969. Verrecchia's ice cream parlour (left of the railway station) was a constant temptation to passers-by (see also p. 103).

Birds' nests in Edwardian Elm Grove.

Fratton Road, with the Co-op and Wesley Central Hall, 1950s.

Queen Street in October 1957, shortly before redevelopment and road-widening took place.

Putting out the flags in Queen Street, *c.* 1906.

High Street, Old Portsmouth, in the 1930s. This area was bombed in January 1941.

Deliveries in Herbert Road, *c.* 1910.

Francis Avenue, *c.* 1910.

Hertford Street, *c.* 1935.

Flooding in Broad Street, undated. Loader's Dining Rooms moved from Commercial Road to 39 Broad Street in the late 1890s and traded there until 1912.

Channel Airways Hawker Siddeley 748 on the Eastern Road, 15 August 1967. Two airliners crashed and slid off Portsmouth Airport's grass runway on this day, but there were no casualties. These incidents raised concerns about the safety of short runways, and contributed to the decline and closure of the airport at the end of 1973.

Four

All Good Children...

A Milton Infant's School class, *c.* 1924.

Unusual class portrait, St. Luke's School, 1930s.

Flying Bull Lane School, built in 1874, is seen here in 1974, two years before its demolition during the redevelopment of Mile End.

A class at Milton Junior Boys' School, with hands ordered out of sight, 1927. Built in 1875 as a mixed school, it was extended in 1906 and boys and girls were separated. The traditional Victorian elements of school architecture are evident here. Notable features include the functional but attractive glossed brickwork (reminiscent of those Victorian underground public conveniences) and high-placed windows (intended to prevent distractions). A well-groomed class like this could mean one of only two things: that either the nit nurse or the photographer was paying a visit. The Portsmouth school nit nurse service was set up in 1919, when it was found that 29.5% of children examined were 'suffering from verminous contamination'. By 1927 the Portsmouth School Medical Officer was able to report that the figure had been reduced to 8.4%. It was reasoned that 'without this constant supervision, children from families who are habitually unclean would speedily become a menace to the cleanliness of all with whom they associate'. Other diseases that were regularly identified during school medical inspections included ringworm, scabies, impetigo and sight and hearing defects.

Portsmouth Training College students at Treloar's Home for Crippled Children, Alton, in the summer of 1924. A charity appeal raised enough money to secure fifty beds at Alton to treat Portsmouth's physically disabled children. There were estimated to be 500 children in the Borough in need of such treatment.

Foster Hall, Teacher Training College, Milton, *c.* 1937.

Gordon Boys' Brigade at Sydney Cottage on the corner of King's Street and Green Road, *c.* 1907. Set up in 1889, the aim of this movement was to help poor and homeless boys earn a living and secure permanent employment. The Harman family ran the Brigade until the Second World War. After its closure and sale, Sydney Cottage became a brothel.

Barefoot child in Edinburgh Road, 1914. In pre-welfare state days it was left to charities and institutions like the Gordon Boys' and St. Faith's Mission Shoeblacks Brigade to do all they could to alleviate poverty by providing temporary work and a warm bed. Such *ad hoc* provision inevitably helped only a few of those in need. Many children in poorer areas went barefoot or wrapped rags around their feet in winter. The setting up of a charity boot fund in 1910 was intended to provide footwear for at least some of the poor children in the borough. Although lucky recipients had warm feet, the stigma of wearing 'Goodwill boots' was keenly felt.

Boys outside the Navy Recruitment Office, The Hard, c. 1905. This photograph was taken by Alfred J. West, the pioneering documentary film maker of Southsea, who has been attributed with inventing the first automatic camera shutter.

Detail from a photograph of munition workers at Hilsea during the First World War. Although a very hazardous occupation, the employment of children was evidently not considered a problem.

Cosmo Lang and Cyril Garbett (seen here
c. 1915) were vicars of Portsea who both went
on to become Archbishop of York. Their work
and influence ensured that St. Mary's became a
model for other Anglican parishes thoughout
the country. Despite his success, Cyril Garbett
was plagued throughout his life by the recurring
nightmare of going to his pulpit on a Sunday
evening to deliver his sermon and finding that
he was completely on his own.

The Inn of Good Fellowship charity soup
kitchen, Kent Street, c. 1930.

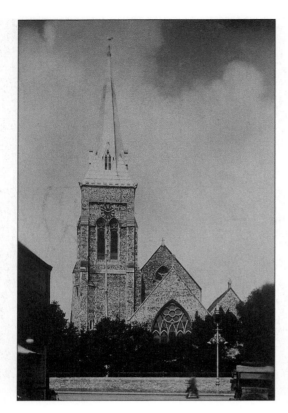

St. Jude's Church, seen here around 1935, was built by housing developer Thomas Ellis Owen in 1851 to induce rich people to move into the expensive villas and terraces which he had built nearby.

Royal Marines form a bridal archway for a high-ranking wedding at St. Jude's Church, undated.

Twyford Avenue Wesleyan Band of Hope Prize Choir, dressed in virginal white in 1912. Mabel Saunders is on the right of the moustached choirmaster.

Band of Hope Maypole Display at Alexandra Park, *c.* 1912.

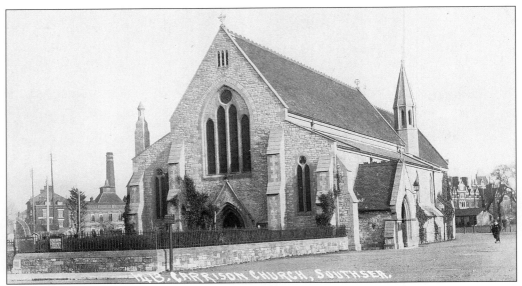

Fine portrait of the Royal Garrison Church, *c.* 1910.

St. Mark's Church, North End, from Laburnam Grove, April 1969. Built in 1874, its slender tower of brick and flint was described as the 'one redeeming landmark in the London Road shopping centre'. It was demolished in the 1970s.

Five

Leisure and Pleasure

Promenaders with parasols on Southsea Common, *c.* 1912.

The swannery on the Canoe Lake, *c.* 1910.

Tom Sadden plays with his train set in the backyard of his Dunbar Road home, *c.* 1922.

Racing model yachts on the Canoe Lake, *c.* 1910.

Donkey rides on Southsea Common, *c.* 1914.

Passing the day on a park bench in Victoria Park, *c.* 1912. Between the wars a 'parliament' of elderly men met in the park to debate the issues of the day.

Fancy-dress street-party in Ranelagh Road, Stamshaw, *c.* 1945. Doris Shaw is in the middle of the fourth row, with a ribbon in her hair, smiling and bending forward. Her friend Gloria Jessup is standing to her right with two hair ribbons. Doris lived at number 108 and Gloria at 110.

Milton Park entrance in Goldsmith Avenue, *c.* 1929.

Swings, see-saws, pedal cars and tricycles at the Canoe Lake in the 1950s.

Roller skating on South Parade Pier, *c.* 1909.

Romantic night-time dancing on South
Parade Pier, *c.* 1920.

Clarence Pier Pavilion in the 1930s.

Hilsea Lagoon in the 1930s.

A walk on the prom in the 1950s. Top radio bands appeared at the Savoy every Friday while the neighbouring Milk Bar (on the right) provided shakes until midnight.

Moderne Bingo Hall, Bradford Junction, 1971. The former Plaza cinema opened in 1929, presented the first 'talkies' in Portsmouth, was renamed the Gaumont in 1931, survived as a bingo hall and was designated a grade II listed building in 1995.

The Empire Theatre, Edinburgh Road, 1958. Opened in 1891, this theatre was known as the Coliseum from 1913 to 1946, but was demolished in the late 1950s.

The Queen's Cinema, Queen Street, 1970. This picture house was opened in 1914 and its location made it a firm favourite with sailors and their acquaintances. It was demolished in the 1980s.

Above: Odeon, Southsea, 1973. Built in 1935 by Andrew Mather, the architecture of this distinctive yellow-tiled cinema captured the spirit of escapism of 1930s Hollywood. The dream ended with demolition in 1985.

The Classic Cinema, Commercial Road, c. 1950. The film *Waterloo Road* starring John Mills and Alistair Sim is billed. The Classic was opened as Cinenews in 1936 and closed in 1972.

This gathering is believed to be in front of George Tutte's beerhouse on the corner of Kingston Road and Malthouse Road, 1909.

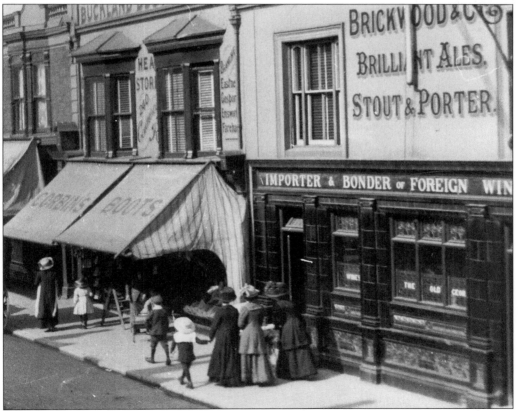

The Old George, Kingston Road, c. 1910.

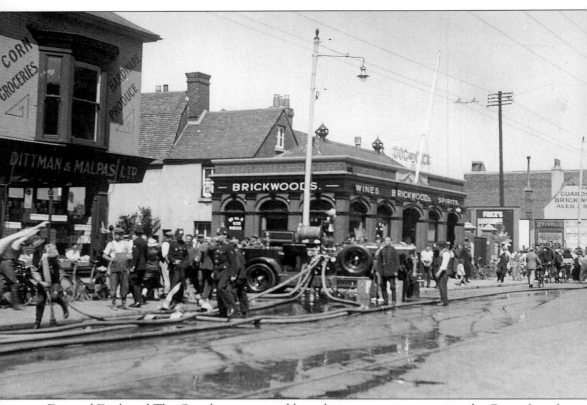

Dog and Duck and The Guardsman pictured here during attempts to put out the Co-op fire of 1934. The Troxy cinema opened on the site between these two pubs in 1936.

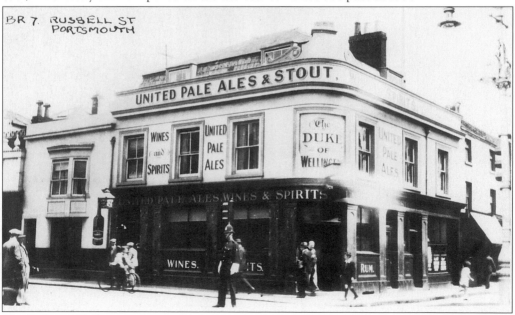

The Duke of Wellington, pictured here between the wars, was on the east side of Russell Street.

The Old Free House, Queen Street, 1958. The premises of wine merchant Owen J. Carter can be seen on the corner of Half Moon Street. The narrow width of Queen Street before redevelopment is evident here.

The Windmill and Sawyer, Copenhagen Street, 1965.

The King and Queen, Cosham High Street, *c.* 1910. This old pub housed its own small brewery.

The Baker's Arms, Holloway Street, *c.* 1907. Holloway Street linked Railway View to Canal Walk.

The Osborne Hotel (left) and the Sailor's Return, Commercial Road, *c.* 1963.

The Old Trafalgar, Fratton Road and Paynes (later Gales) off-licence on the corner of Stamford Street, *c.* 1935.

The Mystery, Somerstown, 1965. This pub, designed by architect A.E. Cogswell, was preserved when the rest of the Plymouth Street area was demolished and now provides a welcome contrast to the council blocks that surround it.

The Golden Bell, on the corner of Amelia Street and Charlotte Street, 1963. This was reportedly a lively pub, popular with sailors and market traders. In the 1950s, passers-by would stand outside and listen to the landlord Edgar Harris playing the piano. Edgar and Lucy Harris left in 1959 and their family has continued to run various pubs in the city.

Dockyard Drillers Football Team, March 1921.

Members of HMS *Vernon* Torpedo School Cycling Club, *c.* 1899. Club expeditions were strictly regulated, with orders being signalled by whistle. No rider was permitted to overtake the Captain.

A crowd of 8,000 gathered at Fratton Park to watch a nil-nil draw against Plymouth Argyle on 11 October 1905. Portsmouth played in pink and were known as 'The Shrimps' until the 1912/13 season when they adopted a more masculine blue.

Pompey, *c.* 1955. Top row, left to right: McGree, Mansell, Gunter, goalkeeper Uprichard, Reid, Pickett, Henderson. Bottom row, left to right: Harris, Gordon, the great Jimmy Dickinson, Rees and Dale.

Portsmouth evidently lost in this game against West Ham at Fratton Park, undated photograph by Stephen Cribb.

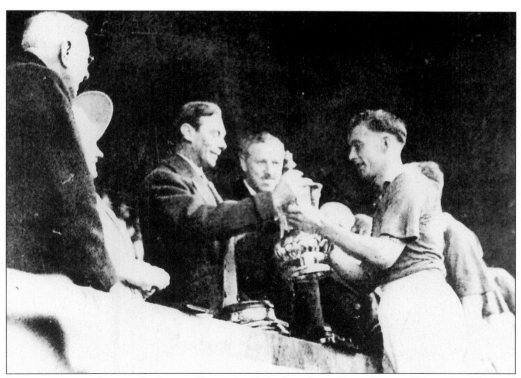

Pompey captain Jimmy Guthrie collects the F.A. Cup from King George VI on the 29 April 1939, after Pompey beat Wolves 4-1 at Wembley.

Messing about in boats at Milton between the wars.

Locks Sailing Club, *c.* 1907. Milton Regatta was started by the Locks Sailing Club in 1908 and included many competitive sports, including rowing, sailing and climbing a greasy pole.

Six
Industry and Trade

Shipbuilding at Vosper-Thorneycroft, the Camber, 1972. Engineer Herbert Vosper purchased Reid's shipbuilding yard in the Camber in 1912. After the Second World War the yard specialised in building high-speed craft.

Portsmouth Power Station, 1965. Built between 1892/4, this was the first publically owned power station in the country to employ a steam turbine. In 1922, the Camber Dock was opened for colliers. The station was demolished in 1984/5.

Twyford Wharf, c. 1950. The privately owned quays of Twyford and Rudmore dealt mainly in coal, fuel oil and sand and ballast. By the early 1970s they handled nearly a quarter of the City's trade.

Drayman and coal cart, Kingston Road, February 1971.

New petrol station in Commercial Road, 1959. The gasometer was built in 1875, bombed in 1940, subsequently repaired, but demolished in 1977.

Portsmouth Times' publisher Holbrook's premises, Commercial Road, *c.* 1909. *The Portsmouth Times* began publication in 1850 but was taken over by *The Hampshire Telegraph* in 1928.

Portsmouth Evening News office in Stanhope Road. The first copy of *The Evening News* was launched from a former butcher's shop in Arundel Street in 1877. Founded by a Scot, James Graham Niven, the first papers were printed and folded by hand and sold for a halfpenny. In 1895 the newspaper moved to these purpose-built premises in Stanhope Road. The present News Centre at Hilsea was built in 1968 by J. Cogswell.

Newsagent Mr Sidney Churchill outside his Commercial Road shop on the day of its closure in July 1972. Mr. Churchill's shop was next door to Darmanin's the hairdresser on the corner of Prince's Street. This part of Mile End was demolished to make way for road-widening and redevelopment in the mid 1970s.

Cobb's the newsagent, No. 5 Bonfire Corner, *c.* 1890. Frederick Cobb ran a grocery shop from these premises in 1897 and, by 1909, Thomas Cobb was in business here as a hairdresser.

Belmonts', the 'costumier, milliner and gown specialist', closing down sale, London Road, October 1970.

Fred Perkins High Class Tailor's shop, Osborne Road, next to Queen's Hotel, c. 1907. Mr Perkins made riding garments for ladies and shooting garments for men. By 1911 he had moved to Palmerston Road.

Hartley's the naval tailor, Commercial Road, *c.* 1912. This business was established around 1880 and had the advantage over its many rivals of being situated opposite the Royal Sailors' Rest.

Mrs Ingersoll, at 83 the oldest totter at the Walls (Unicorn Road) Market, photographed in the summer of 1973. The Unicorn Cafe and Theobald's the tobacconist are visible in the background.

Searching for a bargain at the Walls, 1972.

Scene outside Henry Murphy's stores in Arundel Street, *c*. 1930.

An earlier view of Murphy's shop. In 1932, Henry and Emily Murphy moved their business to North Street in Gosport.

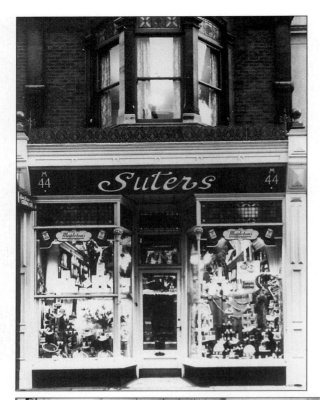

The Suter family high-class grocery business began in Palmerston Road in 1868, but moved to Osborne Road in the 1890s. This photograph was taken shortly after the business was taken over by Mr C.W.J. Savage in 1947. As well as stocking traditional groceries, Mr Savage pioneered the sale of vegetarian and health foods.

Interior of Suters in the 1950s, when weight was imperial, bacon was sliced by hand, coffee was roasted on the premises and the customer was offered a chair while her order was personally satisfied.

Mr Savage (left) and Mrs Savage (centre, suited) and their staff and families about to embark on a staff outing in the 1950s.

The off-licence in Malins Road, 1973, prior to extensive redevelopment of the area.

Signwriter George Dick outside his business in Forbury Road, *c.* 1930. Having served his apprenticeship with George Figgings in the 1890s, George Dick established a high quality sign firm which continues to this day, having been passed down to his grandson, Bill.

The skill of the signwriter is clear, however unhealthy the message, on this property on the corner of Hyde Park Road and Telegraph Street in the 1930s.

Above: At work in George Dick's workshop in the 1930s. The company moved with the times and by 1938 was advertising 'Neon Tube Installations – Schemes in Radiant Neon for Every Business'.

'Give us a W'! Installing the Brickwoods sign on the Sussex Hotel in the 1950s.

Flemings of Castle Road, *c.* 1910. In 1914 there were 31 licensed pawnbrokers in Portsmouth as well as many other similar establishments offering the same service – a semi-respectable means of borrowing cash.

Fulljames' pawnbroking sign over Arundel Street, 1968. In the last century, Fulljames ran a pawnbroking business in Fratton Street and, by the late 1930s, the family operated another branch in Highland Road. Relative affluence and the success of the welfare state contributed to a decline in the trade and, by the late 1960s, Fulljames – the last pawnbroker in Portsmouth – closed down. The trade has been revived in the city in the 1990s.

Lennies' second-hand goods shop in St. Mary's Cresent, 1972.

Ben Grubb's Commercial Road shop, seen here in the 1960s, sold government surplus stores and salvage stock, including ex-military haversacks which were very popular with schoolboys after the war. Grubb's emporium moved down Commercial Road to premises next to The Country House pub, but closed in the 1970s.

H. Samuel's public clock, Commercial Road, 1930s. Amongst other shops visible here are Bateman's the optician, Lennards the boot makers, Home and Colonial Stores and Pickett's, all of which were destroyed in the war. Samuel's installed a new clock on its rebuilt premises.

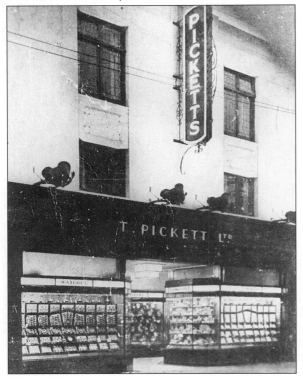

T. Pickett's the jewellers, illuminated in Commercial Road, c. 1937. Established in 1850, by the 1930s there were two Pickett's shops in Commercial Road and another in Elm Grove. Pickett's later joined with John Purser to form Pickett and Purser.

Mr Bridge is believed to have run this small business in Lake Road in the 1930s.

Bailey and Whites, timber importers, Mile End, 1966. Established in 1899, this company also imported slate and other construction materials, and ran a brickworks at Burrfields Road.

The Arcade, Edinburgh Road entrance, *c.* 1907. Amongst the traders in the Arcade at this time were Andrews' Portmanteaus, Dress Basket and Bag Manufacturers and Bartlett's Toy and Fancy Bazaar. Swiss immigrants Baptiste and Bartholomew Albertolli arrived in Portsmouth in 1893 and built up the very successful Swiss Cafe business.

Madden's Handyman Restaurant, Unicorn Road, *c.* 1907. Mr Madden was an ex-sailor whose no-nonsense meals were appreciated most when the fleet was in.

The illuminated fascade of Verrecchia's, London Road, *c.* 1950 (see also p. 49).

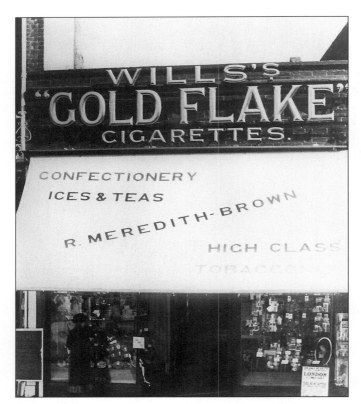

Ralph Meredith-Brown ran this tobacconist and sweet shop at No. 3 Victoria Road South from the late 1920s. Photographer Edgar Ward had previously worked from these premises (see Section 8).

Harrow Stores, Commercial Road, pictured in 1971 shortly before demolition.

A.E. Pascoe, fishmonger, Queen Street, *c.* 1915. Other fish merchants of this period were Burgess, Hooper and Slape. Next door to Pascoe's is Gieve, Matthews and Seagrove, naval tailors.

Knight's of 57/61 Castle Road, the place to go for film for your Box Brownie in the 1930s.

Arthur Cadman's bicycle shop, 279 Arundel Street, 1970. In the 1920s, a similar business was run on these premises by Meek and Co., until Cadman's was established in around 1930.

Timothy White's, Highland Road, *c.* 1968. This national chain had its origins in the mid nineteenth century when a Portsmouth chemist, Timothy White, set up a shop in Union Street. By 1968 there were over 600 branches, but the company was bought out and absorbed by its main competitor, Boots, seen here waiting to pounce.

Seven

PIMCO – The Success of Co-operation

Birthplace of the Co-operative movement in Portsmouth, a cornershop in Charles Street, which opened in May 1873, but soon proved too small to satisfy demand. As can be seen here, the shop was later occupied by a barber.

Co-operative House in Fratton Road was opened in 1937 and boasted a pneumatic cash tube system, Australian walnut and macassar ebony counters and a luxury restaurant on the top floor. It was bombed in January 1941, but rebuilt after the war.

John Jacques, later Lord Jacques of Portsea Island, 1953. John Jacques was Chief Executive of the Portsea Island Mutual Co-operative Society (PIMCO) from 1945 to 1965, during which time he helped double membership and increase sales six-fold. His forward thinking led to the introduction of many revolutionary concepts, including Britain's first fully self-service store at Albert Road in 1948. He entered the House of Lords in 1968, taking his title out of respect for the community he had served so well in business and as a JP. Lord John or 'JJ', as he was known in the city, died in 1995 at the age of 90.

Bread and coal delivery vehicles, *c.* 1937. What is believed to have been the first co-operative society in Britain was set up in Portsmouth in 1796 by dockyard workers who were fed up with being ripped-off by local tradesmen. The aim of the early co-operators was to offer an alternative by organising and controlling the production and distribution of goods and services under a system operated by and for the people. The Portsea Island Mutual Co-operative Society, set up by a handful of volunteers in a rented cornershop in 1873, moved to purpose-built premises in Besant Road five years later and by the late 1880s had established an impressive store in Fratton Road with grocery, boots, drapery and bakery departments and stables. Despite hostile opposition from landowners, local politicians and private tradesmen, PIMCO went from strength to strength, opening branches all over the borough and beyond. Shocked by the extent of milk adulteration and profiteering in the dairy industry, the Society diversified into dairy farming and the Co-op milk delivery was born. Though most famous for its milkman and the 'divi', the Co-op has also contributed much to the social, cultural and educational life of Portsmouth for over a hundred years.

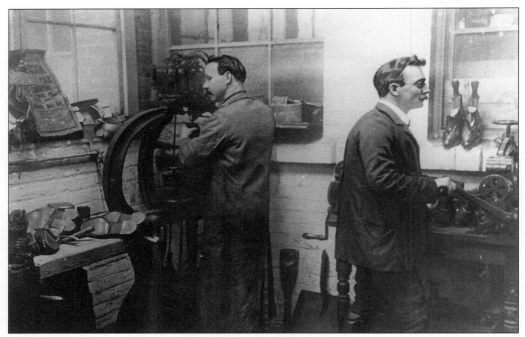

Footwear repairs, *c.* 1910.

The boots and shoes department in Fratton Road, *c.* 1910.

Ice-cream seller Cyril Bryan in Copnor Road in the 1930s, when ice-cream lived up to its name.

Paulsgrove, c. 1950. After the war, mobile grocers and butchers shops were employed to serve the new estates before permanent branches could be built.

The tailoring department, *c*. 1910.

Fire drill at Fratton Road, *c*. 1910. A fire in 1934 destroyed the original Central Co-op premises in Fratton Road (see p. 76).

Social and promotional event at the White House grounds in Milton, c. 1910. The junior school is in the background.

Grocery Warehouse in Somers Road North, 1935.

Doorstep milk delivery in the 1930s.

Dairy workers in the 1920s.

Co-op Dairy in Copnor Road, 1930s.

Milk delivery in Shadwell Road in the summer of 1972.

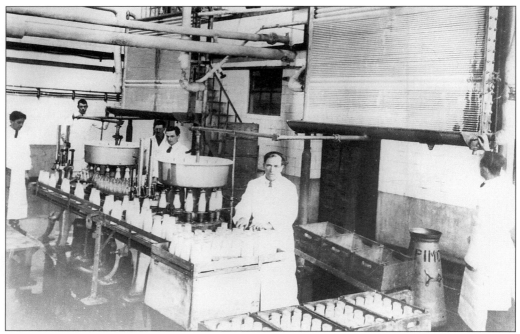
Copnor Dairy in 1929 with, left to right: Mr Vile, Mr Abraham, Mr Pocock, Mr Shepherd, Mr James and Mr Broomfield.

Main grocery store in Fratton Road shortly after its opening in 1933.

Eight

Beside the Sea

On Southsea Beach in the 1920s.

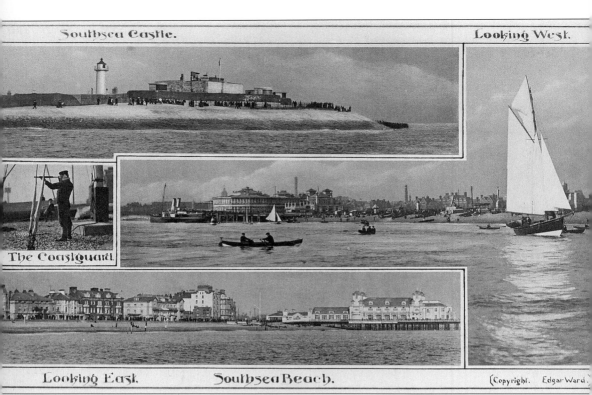

Southsea Castle.   Looking West.

The Coastguard.

Looking East.   Southsea Beach.   (Copyright. Edgar Ward.)

Southsea photo-montage, *c.* 1911, by Edgar Ward, a superb seaside and night photographer who ran his business from 3 Victoria Road South (see also p. 104).

South Parade from the pier, *c.* 1906.

Clarence Pier, *c.* 1911, by Edgar Ward. The concert pavilion on the left offered vocal concerts, sacred music and military bands throughout the season.

Clarence Pier, 1920s. Charabancs deposited excited members of works outings and family groups at Clarence Pier for a day of sun, sea and tacky pleasures.

Southsea Castle, Beach and Promenade, by Edgar Ward, *c.* 1912.

A walk on the prom *c.* 1910. South Parade Pier had recently been rebuilt by talented local architect G.E. Smith (see also p. 15).

Bathing machines and paddlers in a view from South Parade Pier, *c.* 1909. Lumps Fort and Eastney Barracks are visible on the skyline.

Playing on Southsea's stony beach, *c.* 1909.

Isle of Wight steamer at Clarence Pier, *c.* 1910. Like many other piers, Clarence was originally built as a landing and departure point for ferries.

Isle of Wight steamers the *Solent Queen* (at the pier), the *Duchess of Fife* (leaving) and the *Lord Kitchener* (in the distance).

Airliner over Southsea, 1930s. This alternative means to cross the Solent was first offered by the Portsmouth, Southsea and Isle of Wight Aviation Company in the summer of 1932. Four flights were made a day with a single fare costing six shillings and a return, ten shillings.

Rare aerial view taken in the mid 1930s, looking towards Portsmouth Harbour. Landmarks include the YMCA, the Cathedral and, on the right, the Victoria Barracks.

Rare view of Old Portsmouth by Edgar Ward, *c.* 1912. Advertisers jostled for the attention of sailors as they arrived in the busy port with money to spend.

Yachting in the Solent by Stephen Cribb, a local and naval photographer who added hydroplanes to some of his photographs to improve composition and add interest.

Furling and stowing the head sails on board naval training ship *St. Vincent* in Portsmouth Harbour, *c.* 1903.

Beached paddle steamer the *Duchess of Kent* at Old Portsmouth, after colliding with the S.S. *Transporter* on 3 September, 1909.

Portsmouth Harbour, 1864. A shipyard is visible in the foreground of this early view across the mouth of the harbour looking towards Blockhouse Fort, soon to be established as a sea-mining base.

Old buildings at Point, just before demolition in the 1960s.

Fishermen at the Camber, *c.* 1950. Portsmouth's importance to the fish trade was almost solely as a distribution centre in the 1950s, though a small but successful fleet was working by the 1980s. In the early years of the century, the catch was landed at the old Point market. Local fishmongers waited for the boats to come in at four in the morning, nursing a tuppenny measure of rum and coffee in the Still and West.

The Camber during the Arctic conditions of January 1963. Langstone Harbour and Fareham Creek froze over and ice up to four feet thick was reported. When the thaw came, some boats which were embedded in the ice were carried out to sea and never seen again.

In Remembrance. The War Memorial Gateway at the Royal Hospital in Commercial Road was opened by Princess Helena Victoria on the 19 May 1922 to perpetuate the memory of the thousands of local men killed in the First World War. More than a third of the men who joined the Portsmouth Battalions are known to have been killed, though numbers wearing the uniforms of other regiments and the total of sailors and marines drawn from the area are not known. An incomplete list of five thousand names was submitted for inclusion in a Roll of Honour. The memorial was dismantled in 1969.

Rest in Peace. Mile End Cemetery collonade, 1957. This cemetery was established in 1831 by the Portsea Island General Cemetery Company and occupied four acres of land between Wharf Road and Kettering Terrace. Nearly 30,000 people were buried there before it was conveyed by a Deed of Gift to the City Council in 1958 and converted into Mile End Gardens in the early 1960s. The land, which a restrictive covenant ensured should be left as an open space in perpetuity, is now part of the Continental Ferryport.